king of
the fireflies

king of
the fireflies

For Sister Monica Clare -
(aka Claudette) -
we have shared some
amazing times. I look
forward to more perhaps
ongoing of the sacred
and secular. In both
friendship and in
christ -
              x Rebecca
                  10-13-2021

poems by Rebecca Weiner Tompkins

SENSITIVE SKIN BOOKS

Published in the United States by **SENSITIVE SKIN BOOKS**.
Mill Valley, CA

First Edition

SENSITIVE SKIN BOOKS
www.sensitiveskinmagazine.com
www.facebook.com/sensitiveskin

Library of Congress Control Number: 2018959236

ISBN: 978-0-9961570-6-3

Some of these poems were published previously in *Intro,
Poetry magazine, Seneca Review, Pequod, Ploughshares,
Anthology of American Verse & Yearbook of American Poetry, 1986–
88 ed., The Antioch Review, A Poetry Collection, NYU,1991,
The Mercury Reader, Sensitive Skin magazine*

For my beloved departed: Jack, Gloria, Charlie, JoAnn, and Deborah
and those newly arrived: Louis and Florence

CONTENTS

ONE 1

TWO

THREE   41

FOUR   61

FIVE

ONE

NATURE LESSON

I don't know what's inside
this once new black walnut. Someone picked it
unmarred and bright from the wet ground,
said: *smell this*. I had to press it
to my nose. After five days on the table,
the wrinkling, speckling seed or shell—which,
I couldn't tell—had changed. The tough skin, today like a
spoiling lime, has kept guarding
the tang of damp woods in fall, burnt and shady,
while also greenly still alive, yet even that scent
has faded farther in. What I'd like
is to carve this open with a small, sharp knife. If
the heart can't reveal its own secret being,
nothing can, and now
this shriveling globe, its center hidden,
offers only faint clues and tiresome supposition. I'm
holding this roundness right in the curve
of my palm; it's not enough. Here's the first
cut. Watch closely.

AFTER YOU SAID I ALWAYS LOSE THINGS

The red birthstone fell
out of my ring, leaving
its crowned prongs empty,
a perfect chip chiseled
from my heart's bones.

I dreamed being stopped by
the long dark walkway
with bricked wall leading
to the locked iron gate enclosing
the fenced stairwell topped
by the steel door
beside sealed heavy
draped windows, all
now forbidden.

The sweet, sharp birdsong
outside the room you loved
comes at me—
as it's surely been said before—
a barbed fist to the chest,
hooks and lodges in that space
the lost ruby left.

MOURNING NOT A MYTH

Every morning the still new absence
drops like a stone out of your sleep
onto your chest, heart and lungs, the parts
you need to begin a day,
and sinks you.

Even without turning toward you
I feel its presence
sometimes a flattening slab, others
a speed slamming cannonball.

Here again? I want to ask, to
pat its cool familiar surface in greeting,
but I know it is
inscrutable, and of course
silent as the rock it is, no answer will ever
come, and as it is also
immoveable, not even a budge.

The buoyant miracle in the world outside
of a small sparrow sipping from a tiny puddle
left from the night's drenching
is not enough
to fly away that Sisyphean weight,
to float you up
to life's lift again,
not just yet.

NOT

The deer are not angels. They are not
your father waiting at the edge
of the midnight woods, to say goodbye before
with a kick of his hooves he sets off for good,
or worse, stares with sad eyes
as you drive away and leave him there
finally as alone
as he feared.
At the field's bend
off the road, the deer seem to be waiting
to take you somewhere, as the mist
that rises from the wet grass
around them parts so you
can see their faces, turned back
toward you, catching and holding
your own gaze, distracting you from
the drive in the dark you must make.
You say they look like spirits. They are not;
even when you dream them later
surrounding you with their imploring look,
they're not.

LANDSCAPE WITH BEAR IN IT SOMEWHERE

The limber late light
travels across the ridge
where the bear climbed.
Even with my head thrown back
I still can't take in the tops
of the tall pointed trees
up there. A friend's death
is flickering in and out
of my mind the whole time
I'm watching the yellow binding
weave slowly, lower and lower
down the slope of dusk-deepening
green and I expect the bear
to reverse his way,
track back down
to us, to give
a faster swipe of darkness
to the day's last lit edge
draining any hope I had
that this dying
would not happen
again.

DOG LEAPING IN THE AIR!

How quickly the appeal of
abandon, abandon
becomes to
abandon…be abandoned.

The lost chord
the found note
the open door:

the bird sung
sings morning
multiple cadence
simple scale
enters like an arrow of urgency
but softened.

BAIT

We two friends smell lake
in the air at evening, recall
childhood fishing days, night-
crawlers writhing in styrofoam cups
of sweet black earth. One of us calls it
worms' breath, the scent that after rain
draws the robins to feast.
What draws us to breathe the underground
come up to stretch? There's the old joke
of our only company at death, grotesque
wiggle devouring all that's left. This inhale
of appreciation is like *inspiration*
from the Greek: it fills and feeds us
as we bring it in and speak its voice
if for only an instant,
then shrug it off with a shiver,
think to ditch it like the sprawl of road kill
left after some driver's reckless night,
a family of raccoons garnishing both
shoulder and center line. For us,
speeding past, that's death no flippant twitch
can do away with. No one buries or even
drags the bodies, as if the touch of sympathy
contaminates. Now here we are, oblivious that
swallows have yielded to swooping bats, and
we're smiling so serenely at memory's recognition
of the undulating, peat-colored lives
we once cut into unstilled bloodless segments,
fitting the hook to such perfection
even we would fall for that seamless bait.

CONVERSION

I
Three times the light
happened. First
was in the long room
with so many—some already
dead—and me,
swaddled tight, twisting
my head but the distance
seemed so distant.
My father and
a doctor leaned down
into that bright circle
that pinned me.
Was it not cancer
their gestures meant
or something else
I couldn't quite get; what was it
they mouthed, that shouting
with no sound?

II
Later on—
the next day or another night?—
I tried to sleep in a
shifting sea of beds,
white-sheet bodies turning and
moaning all around me. The light
came on around others
and curtains were pulled
that never covered everything
I shouldn't have seen, a man's
last cry, arms keeping him

from sinking, or was it
rising. On my raft of
darkness I clung to the
winding lines of a song
I once sang, even when
the tune was gone from my ears.
A nurse turned the whole place
fluorescent.
How gray the others were. I was
the only one she washed and
she gasped at the blood
I later heard had almost run out
and now stayed stuck
to my neck where
it had pooled and dried. All
her sponges and powders
couldn't rub it off.
I preferred the still-calling
dark to the hands that tried
to turn me and take me and
make me clean but
knew I shouldn't go back.

III
Then morning,
as I saw the windows and outside
the pink early sky and ice-
blue river, buildings brightening: a first
true dawn. My father was standing
by the metal bed rail. I could almost hear
his voice. Worry spilled
in his eyes, then relief as
my tube-tangled words finally opened:
people died, I heard them
right next to me;

in the day's real light only
neatly tucked linens remained.
The blood they gave me
didn't take, so more came back
into my vein, as the dark would again,
and at last
I stood and
moved my feet
and walked toward the new world
that was clearly waiting.

MAYDAY, MAYDAY

The white rain of petals that fell for a week is done.
What catches now in my hair
are the dried blossoms of the Callery Pear,
startling and crackly, as they float and scatter,
rattling through the trees to the street like
shards of bone sifted in dusty fingers
out of old earth. A young man I know is visiting
his wife's grave a year after she died
and when he tells me his stories of what
the time has been—"where is your wife now?"
people ask; "dead," he replies—his recollecting
is what saves me from another sigh for my recent
tiresomely trite grief, the mundane details of my life
which even led me to write: *I want to stab myself in the heart*
with a knife. It was that simple and stupid
as I woke up every day newly alone.

This morning after, those falling finished flowers,
the papery circles, parchment yellow, are deep
in the gutters and sidewalk gashes.
They're so turned, so far removed from
the handfuls of fresh ones I once threw into
the night air and tried to run through
as they drifted sweeter than stars or first snow.
I am the only one out this early and surprised
to see a small figure, a woman who seems to be
picking through trash, but is actually
crouching outside the iron gate sweeping up
piles of the stiff petals into a sack.
Later she might sort and sell them
in another part of the city as a special tea, a remedy

for heartbreak, or the slightly different heart-
ache, urging those who long for a cure not to resist
the sharp taste, terrible and familiar, going down.

ANOTHER AUTUMNAL

Sometimes I imagine
parking lots are water, dark seas
no longer dry ground
but not either anywhere to drown.
Sometimes all the trees in the park
are radiant yellow
in the end of November twilight,
almost gold, unearthly
under the moist glowy streetlight.
There isn't red or orange or russet,
just that one-colored shimmer of brightness
seemingly in flight.
Sometimes after the leaves finally leave,
the fire escape with the missing slats
appears to be the same color as
the distant emptied treescape;
sometimes it's better to leap
out into unknown branches than
that broken iron opening up only
to what's below.

A WEE GIFT AGAINST DEATH

—For J

Rabbit in the hat:
no sleight of hand this all is.
Look right inside. He's really in there.
I give you this toy that keeps
the rabbit safe and very still.
We don't want to let the magic
escape, let alone dazzle our lives
into unbearable joys.
Then it might be like the rabbit
who makes it to the moon to avoid
the cat in the deep summer grass
of a perfect poem I've read.
We could live in that steady rabbit light.

GETTING IT RIGHT

"If there's any substitute for love it's memory.
To memorize, then, is to restore intimacy."
—Joseph Brodsky

Sometimes the lit wick of a candle
flickers fast like a stroboscope, faster
than the flutter of lashes, so fast
that furniture in a room continues to wobble
when someone new going to sleep beside you
snuffs the flame. What you're seeing
looks the same as when inviting landscape shimmers
in the distance, when the sun's heat
hangs between you and your oasis, and you stumble onward
drawn to that undependable world.
You've got to get it right, not turn away,
as with memory which does this wavering trick
best of all, being something you can't put a literal finger on.
So lying against the sleeper's back
you blink and blink to find what's left, to bring it
clearer, closer, fixed in place. No matter how you stare
at what's been, it's skittish as mirage:
glance away, it's changed. But you don't mind
the game, how the mind's eye blurs an inner sense,
blurs it into any kind of sense
it might make outside, attaching itself to objects
in the room where at least it has the chance of unreality
turning back into reality, as the walls, clock, curtains,
faltering in candlelight and remembered candlelight
will at daylight regain their shapes, until
they've come back, solid and sensible again,
without distortion. You can move up close,
and you can touch them.

DEAD MAN'S FLOAT

Meet me tonight on the far bank
of the Neversink River. At the stillest hour
between needling of cicada and scratch
of cricket there'll be a long stretch of time
until new light opens and the soft moan of doves
rejoins the steady whoosh of wind in the trees.

This river's just begging for it. Not one
soul has ever seen the bottom, despite
that clearest, most silver green of waters.
We can look straight down, and down so deep,
but not a thing slams our eye, or darkens it to ground.
So out of dusk's mild air, dive in: the diagonal swim
is endlessly cool. It seems we could make it through to
some opposite surface, where, as on the globe's other side
spun round in the teacher's hand, for someone else, submersion
is just beginning. Instead, such lovely suspense of the vertical
glide, and suspension of what can't be the next-to-last
stroke, since there is no last one. We'll put it to the test.
If this place proves true to its name, no lack of breath
will let us really fall. With no final floor for any
landing, this smoothest plunge can't ever fail.

WALKING TOWARD ME

When the fireflies switch on
you're the king; they trace
your shape like a giant halo.
The dahlias in the garden
still pop pinkly in the twilight,
now with its yellow and green highlights
of these bugs kids capture
in rattle-lidded jars or squeezed tight fists
to hold the glow. It sifts out
like water or sand they want to
scoop from summer's days and not let
go. This is how you
come to me at the fold of hours
into dusk. I've been waiting.

TWO

WATER

In Maillol's *The River* the sculpted woman
arches at the edge of the pool, while her hair
snakes to the water where rain plunges and splashes.
She lies there with absolute abandon in the wet
evening, as she will in dapples of sunlight when
the water waits calm and reflective. You admire
her. *Abandon, abandon:* the words elongate and
expand; they are the object of your admiration
yet what you fight in yourself, and tell *control,*
control. The flood's forced back, clouds are heavy;
for how long, then what release?

In the museum you stand before the pond
of Monet's waterlilies, and breathe its peace
like a buffer between you and the world. It is
what you believe you desire. These flowers with water
may seethe, yet their deep colors leave you content.
And against this wall of window, far enough away,
you certainly will not drown. Outside the glass, below,
the bronze spreads on her side, elbows bent, palms open, body
an arc of passion, to an invisible, but apparent, partner.
Her eyes and mouth mirror ecstasy in the grace of the moment.
If she seems to be falling to the green surface, her face is flung
fully up, toward the dense dangle, another green, of the weeping
beech. From rain or anything, it does not protect her
with its wide, draping cover. You can see perfectly
how she tilts in every direction, receiving it all from
earth to sky. You see this from inside where you've stayed dry.

PLAYING PUCCINI AND VERDI

The heroines of the great operas
keep dying. There sings not love unrequited
or unfound, but misunderstood, foiled,
betrayed. Mimi, Desdemona, Violeta—
their voices break and soar and ache
in final deathbed arias. They know
what love is, as does Aida in the tomb
or Tosca on the parapet. Sometimes, lucky,
they die in their heroes' arms, breaths uniting
in false hope of second chance, of afterlife.
Single words, though Italian, speak to us:
mio, amore, morire, sogni, addio, sempre
tua, mia vita, saying simply *mine, love, death,*
dream, goodbye, always yours, my life.
When finally tardy realization arrives,
too late to save the lovers, then
how the audience leaps, applauds, weeps, yet
feels at least those are others: unfair victims
of unyielding fate.
Ah, but that truest kiss—
the last—lingers in song. We hear it
again and again; the moment rises, thrilling
with obvious loss and pain. The doomed note
cries *amore,* even as its music slips away.
We crave that theme, listening to the fade;
for us its cause remains dreamed, in hiding.

ANGEL

The angel perches on the church spire
and his wings shine silver
in the morning light. He is a man
who has been a boy all his life,
an eternity of watching others burn like
the mortals in Keats's ode on the urn.
This angel leans down over
the bustling town, its citizens
hurrying forward, eyes gone oblivious,
glued to the ground. He seems ready
to take the plunge, exchange his perfect
stance for a more ordinary and sweaty dance.
He doesn't want to miss that same
fevered kiss the shepherd and his nymph
were deprived of. Though humans
have forgotten how longing lets them
continue, he still knows it's true.
Sweeping low, he searches the faces
for the one he'll call love. When he does,
this desire will show him what to do.

COASTAL ALARM

You meet a man. You find
he fills you with desire:
you're possessed as by a

red speedboat careening
wildly on a crash course
through frenzied dark waters.

It leaves in its churned wake
white-capped waves, killer tides.

You watch your own body
now like some flattened shore

in the path of poisons
washing up; in danger
of seas rising toward it,
dragging it out to drown.

THIS UNNAMED GOD

Call them what you will, with
their two names each, the god
and goddess of Love, Venus
and her son Cupid, of the Romans,
first Aphrodite and Eros from the Greek.
They had power over just that: love.
Meanwhile, sex was not the province
of some other deity, separate
as we now have it, that without
anything else. Then, when the boy
aimed and shot his arrow, its effect
included every aspect of passion, all
deepest feeling, beyond desire and delight.

Recall how Aphrodite, the only
Olympian with no mother or father,
came out of the sparkling sea, and
went back periodically to refresh her
pure and youthful spirit. She rose, truly
marvelous and distinctive in birth, unlike
the other rulers of the dominions
of being; if emptied of her plans and presence
the world could not continue. So why do we think
we've found a better way: no feeling but
the body, thoughtless, perhaps sublime,
often just absolute touch and take.
Even when we hear the whistling
approach of that bow's ammunition
we duck and hurry out of the way. What
we've chosen was given no immortal
name. Yet we imagine without commitment
we've been saved from mortality or mere age.

Remember though, it was love's beautiful
waters that each year brought Aphrodite
renewal, furthered the pleasure of her long days.

DISTANCE

Big city nights but the same air
as anywhere, sweet with spring, soft
with full moon's light. The bicycles are out
swooshing by, the spokes' silver clicks
going round, over and over. From your terrace
you see into lit windows of lives, and
feel this as a lonely time:
border of two seasons, with the unknown
of a new summer ahead. You know
there'll be heat. Yet all the rest
beyond temperature, less clothes, longer days,
won't come to you. You sit up here in the dark
above the street, racking your memory
for clues. You can remember other times:

the cool grass in a field along the ocean,
and someone laughing with you while
you lay together, happy; or standing at the rail
of a ferry coursing the bay, with no destination
except into the sweeping breeze, as you
turned to another with a smile
at the air's clean smell around you; and even
walking home from a party, then stopping
to back against a building and kiss
because at that instant it was all
either of you wanted. These were scenes
with different people, and there have been
more, each one wrapped with you in
moments you still recall. But what was once

is never like what will be. If the summers
of past twist your heart for lost

loves and places, that's only for a distance
you fear: that you'll be leaning over, looking down
to where the riders below whir by, some of them
singing, not one of them glancing up.

BIOLOGY LESSON

The tiny white belly of
the child's dead frog softens
in the bottom of its plexiglass
tank. See how it almost glows,
ugly and loveable as the world
itself. Back to the real, where
your own despair, of not the gone
but the unborn, throws you
to the tiles, that floor
cool and relentless as comfort
should seem. Here's how love
hurts you most: sneakily,
raw and pillow like the
frog's stretch of skin. It's
sunk down, defenseless and
endangering, as the possible
life scheming inside your
own round, soft being. Soon
you'll have to spill it away,
that amphibious flick
of tissue. Soon when he, the child,
asks, you'll say: *it just went,*
not mentioning the flush
or squash and dissolve
of slippery cells so quickly
turned to trash.

NIGHT RIDE

More restless than local teens
cruising their one-block turf,
we're out for all the air we can find.
This man I love drives steady and cool,
elbow hanging casual
on the seatback beside me. And I
let my hair fly, prop my feet
on the dashboard, and smile. Tonight
I'm wearing the dress he likes:
blue; wind rushes by
that same deep shade.
We hunt speed,
the car shooting off on back roads, its motion
making the countryside roar
even above the engine.
That noise doesn't break
into syllable or silence. It's easy, and
we're riding
nowhere, taking each turn
like it meant
somewhere, like it meant a place
waiting, like home.

SUMMER STORM

The couple
closed behind curtains
can't tell if it's wind
or water wrenching the trees.
The noise: first, like
flooded skies rushing down, then
like wild wrap of woods trapped in
the bend of fastest sound.

Two lying as one, listening.
I'd hate to lose you
now, the way a heavy crush
of topmost branches quick snaps
and crashes to ground. Think how
dead things plant obstacles.

That's what you've said
about love: an encumbrance,
it toughens the trail. Yet
it's that difficult delight
that brings us here together. And
if things fall still alive,
they spring back, not to the exact
same place, but to one as plainly
part of the pattern, fit into the
foliage, always swaying dangerously.

SEASONAL

Under a wild autumn evening
of wind-shifted clouds, a woman
meets a man, who could be her lover.
Above them, turmoil races calm
in the weather. A flick of ember
blown from a cigarette turns and flashes
then blinks out in the street. How quick,
she thinks, and strong air whips
through her hair. He could be her
lover, but isn't, or isn't yet. This is
what she gets for settling for
something, and someone, else:
always sensing some other spark, and
how, if fanned, it might
blow up, setting fire to the dark. Or
then again it might be snuffed before
it ever flared. Which wins out she doesn't
know: the sky wrestles within itself
and the ground swallows up any light
that lands. She tilts her head from
up to down, as if to let chance decide
where she'll be found when he bends
to offer her his face, to take hers,
and then, the ready kiss....

GETTING LATE

And wishing you home, I step outdoors
and discover fresh clouds, big and backlit
by a ripening moon. Down between zero
and freezing, the night knocks
right up inside me, slips sharp
inside. If this is what you're out in
no need to save for you the recollection
of the hour's bite. You'll know it too.
But waiting after midnight I imagine
all you find to keep you. In this kind
of cold, everything's paralyzed: cars stall,
stars don't blink, bodies lock, and that which is
most visible—breath—shows up, actually speaks
to another. That warmest part rushes out,
floating in light but true living color. Someone else
could almost hold it in two hands. No doubt
how much that warmth can help. I watch my own air
more faint, and unmet
by any mouth answering back, only
mid-December's cruel and awakening slap.

THE WELL-MADE BOX

Let me tell you more about that box:
when the magician finally
slides the two halves
back in place, and slowly lifts the lid,
Poof
the dazzling girl is gone. Waiting
in the wings, the one in the shiny
new cape steps forward to grab
the empty diadem
and all her spangles trickle
to the floor, their unexpected *clunk*
clunk clunk, surprising like lead slugs
thrown at the stage. The showman
stands alone with his mistakes.

MANGOES AND BLOSSOMS

You stood before them,
the beautiful women of Tahiti.
I loved you more than ever then.
The moon outside the museum rose between buildings.
I took our photo in fuzzy streetlight.
On the bus we sat smiling
across the aisle from each other.
It was our anniversary; it seemed
we were not unhappy.
You bought a bottle of grappa
to recapture some long lost feeling
and began your own rise
and our fall. I should have known
that the paradise of that painting
would escape us once more.

COSTS

I'll give you this,
but I'll take your mother.
That was the answer
to my prayer for that lover,
to build his nest in my heart.
So she has to go
and who knows if that flutter
will stay
or with a feathery rush
fly far away.

No worries can find you,
is my guarantee
were the words that I won
in a trade for my being.
Living such peace with no pain
but no pleasure
leaves not much of life
and the box that held treasure stays
empty, though I'd stored so much
there when believing
I'd keep what I'd found.

STRIKE/STRUCK/STRICKEN

Death unites us again
as it divides us from the loved one
taken too soon of course.
The face of a rare orange cardinal
startles close at the glass
while a rust-capped hawk
tops the lone tree's highest branch.
We want those birds to be the beloved
bringing back a message of how it is,
how it will be when
death unites us again.

THREE

MUSEUM LANDSCAPES

Finally the world without
interference, the world we want given
to us: every scene both low and tall enough
for climbing out of here, into
the luminous views, composed so, of
pinks, yellows, violets, blues.
We come to these paintings
the way a child extends his arms up
wordlessly, with certainty, to be lifted.

Each picture, backed off from,
changes from its strokes and scrapes
of palette and texture, into vision
we'd make our own. And standing
at gallery center, looking
over a shoulder, forward, behind, we're surrounded
by places where we place ourselves, say we've
surely once been or dreamed or still would be.

Stare through the bright surfaces; we are
there, not merely wishing, or could
be. Why should we live only
in rooms where light is measured
for careful letting in. See
how these perfect windows open into
where the light's best, with nothing
that gets in its, and our, way.

ANGEL PLAYING THE VIOLIN

Her bare feet,
beneath a skirt of gauzy blue,
float in golden air,
that yellow orange view
bright behind the altar
where high up her song
attends Our Lady above,
herself held,
in a sun-washed circle of sky
shimmering down
its coins of light. They tell us
keep your eyes on the prize,
the heavenly figures
lifted and balanced, buoyant
from heels to elbows to crown.
We long for that invisible hold,
the same lift,
its lit music all around
as we too are carried
way up, our palms
folded, our own feet
so tipped they'd fit
neatly in God's hand.

POEM WITH ONE WORD MISSING

Mid-March in the country,
that late night the thawed world
slept, patchy grasses still,
while inside we curled
in our own breaths and outside
shut blinds, the surprising snow
came on silently, spreading
over everything with its sudden
coat of heavy quiet. Now
we discover morning's usual
brightness piled right up to
our eyes at the window,
the sky seeming like
sun could shine behind
but wouldn't. Instead
the lightest flakes are falling
all coming down
to the only color left, its
feathery close cover not
closing, but holding us too
and we open the door and our
hands and faces, even
our eyes, to know that slight touch
able to change everything, so
much waiting, finally slowed
by this steadiness,
simple,
but of such deep mind.

ELECTRONIC DIALOGUE

I
At my wife's grave
it's changed a lot in a month;
someone's planted some forget me nots.
It's windy and flower petals from the trees are making pink
whirlwinds.

II
I know you're at the grave.
Of course you can imagine my reply to you
standing in the swirling pink falling blossoms...x

III
That is a pretty email. Is it a haiku?
Here's pictures of all the candles from last year and the view from
my balcony. Also the grave today and the petals blowing around
bluebells. Ok, I faked that second one by throwing some in the air.

IV
A true haiku might be:

today at the grave
you imagine my reply:
pink falling blossoms.

That changes who or what it's about
but fits the format and sensibility correctly
and is nicer.
However it can be a poem of two parts.
I might write it.

HOW WE DIE

Death is cumulative;
the bodies pile up—
she tells us her story
of life so far.
I imagine the horizontal stacks
lining the borders
of an endless hall,
the high walls
closing in, as corpses
with ragged edges,
packed and flat,
diminish our long view.
We've seen so many
horror films, how zombies
suddenly
snap upright,
their forlorn faces
gray, unblinking sight
hollow, under eyes black,
and hungry mouths' corners
leaking blood. They want us
to come be with them
as much as to take them back.
Where were we going
anyway? If I once knew,
I forgot.

SOUTHWESTERN

A man meets three
agents of death: lightning
nearly misses the tree; a
pale scorpion sits silent
at the door of his sleep; and
a truck swerves seconds
before it's head-on.
He begins to think
either God is calling him back
to that desert and he needs
to offer himself up, or it could
just be something else, even
nothing. Can one discern
what direction the signs are
pointing if one hates the
idea, the very word, plus
staring at the sun too long
has clouded one's vision?
The man talks it out
endlessly, to the wrong
listeners, shouts it in the
wrong rooms. Does God
want him whole or would he
rather make and take him
broken? What has already
been told: the lost get found
and darkness turns light and
sins can be turned around,
seems old; there's nothing
left to tell or teach. Now
this is where we might
leave him, find another

story, ours, which starts up
almost alike, only the names
or dates have been changed.
God, of course,
remains the same.

FRONT PAGE

In a land of war
a boy has to move fast.
See him hurrying, not
to get caught, his sandals
scuffing up dust in the cracked
street, his canvas bag
clutched to his skinny
chest, above spindly, strong legs.
These legs can hustle
when they have to, which
is ever since he's been
old enough to be told
anything, mostly go. What other life is there
than the death that's always
nearly his, though so far isn't:
the babies blown from their
carriages, the groceries
exploding with the mothers'
arms, the families strewn
across that dry, torn ground.

Across seas, a photo of this boy
might astound citizens reaching
across coffee for another
slice of toast and jam, but doesn't
for too long. He's captive
only for the moment, glancing
furtively around, at what
could be the camera
or more probably
is what follows him
until it will bring him down.
For the breakfasting ones,

the moment turns,
thankfully, with the page. For the boy
it's duplicated in others, children
yet, and children still
when amidst large, useless ruin,
their smaller, as useless,
limbs are found.

WHOSE VICTIM

I

In the shadowy winter woods
that circled the skating pond
a man was watching, had snatched
a girl the evening before and left
her alive but undressed and silent.
We huddled together on the ice
and hurried home at dusk, feeling
the dangerous gloom creep around.
We knew all about it; our mothers
told us, telling us nothing really
but fear that kept us whispering
like they did in the parking lots,
the supermarket, and on the phone.

II

On the beach beneath the eucalyptus
fringed cliffs a man was waiting,
having axed three coeds in the head
while they slept under stars.
We were warned, so put away our own
sleeping bags and came back at dark
to the dorms where we'd be safe behind
our locked windows; he was looking up
from the waves' edge below and would
be all night, crouched
to take any one of us. This time we knew
the details, had seen the photos, told
our mothers we weren't afraid, and were
being careful. We lied, and lay awake
for new reasons for the first time.
This one was after more than underwear,
our mothers had definitely told us.

III

I'm still lying awake,
now in my own apartment.
A man is walking around. I know he's
in the house; it's all I know at night.
A woman, a mother, a wife, I've
learned the worst the world can hold,
but it's finally this terror,
making the floor creak,
sending a shape across the wall,
holding out a hand to grab me, until
I'll scream the way those others did
again and again. Nobody heard them,
my mother, lowering her voice, told me.

DOMESTIC REPORT

A man knows how to shoot
to kill. He's born to bear
the slap of a gun in his
open hand. If he didn't reach
for that power, no matter: it still
fits; he can learn to love it.
A woman is taught to curb the will
to strike out or back. She's
made to cower in fear or crouch
at his feet like an easy target.
They make babies from this
arrangement, created in their image.
The boys collect sticks
for fighting; the girls tend the
sick baby dolls, and endlessly
fix what's to eat. They live
together in the dark, sleep on
beds of boards; some
get beaten while some dole it out.
When the officers come to clear
things up, get to the bottom
of what's gone about, they're
appalled, they tell the press,
"These people aren't human."
The neighbors nod their own shock.
They didn't call, just thought
it was, "you know, a lovers' quarrel,"
never realized there were children
who could live in such a hell.
When they pull the shades
that night on their homey
scene, the fathers shout, the mothers

scream, the kids cry. If you lean
close to listen, don't be surprised
when you hear familiar voices,
find yourself joining in.

LOST FRIENDS

Wake and hear the heavy rain
that mops the night,
dragging the rush of cars along.
If you call to ask her
how she's doing, will she just sigh out
and say: *he beats me now everyday,*
it's best when he's dead, I mean sleeping.
That's not what she wants
to believe, or to feel his reason:
her own fault must be
at the blackest heart of it all.

Think what she's doing now
these same glowing clock hours,
pressing her ears to headphones,
tapped into music, say Wagner,
that bends the possible dark
into something else, like a drape
of rich fabric, not silk but velvet
or satin jacquard, the luxury
a complicated sweep of sound; this
sort of rising emotion she can take.
When and where it takes her
she can bear; these tears come from no
fear or pain she wonders what she did
to bring on, what role she's played.

Keep listening to tonight's rain.
It's the kind that wears away the last
slick of mud and, catching them by the backs
of their necks, sweeps the bodies out to sea.
But she won't be calling you about that

or the other bad feelings that steal her from sleep;
she won't be calling you anymore. What brought her
to your own sleepless mind: you can't find
an answer to that. You don't even know if she's
hearing this rotten weather; does anyone know what
another is thinking, ever?

MISSING

Radio silence sets in.
Who said we seek that solitary songless
and sweetless time? Why would we?
I'm going to stop saying that I do.
Someone played piano for me
and someone once before that, like in two poems
I read where in each a grown man remembers a parent
playing, and himself sitting underneath or next to, the thick strings
vibrating into every chamber of being.
I hear Heart and Soul and then it's my own father's hands with mine.
I hear Scott Joplin and the old and new standards and it's someone
else I'll love. It all fills me up.
Its absence is what
empties me. The dial turned all the way to the right
and not a sound.

THE PAYMENT

Always you feel beautiful in the light.
Is it only sensation you've craved: the body
born to bloom, arcing open beneath the sun,
the smile surrounding your every curve, pore, angle.
For this some say you may have sold your soul.

So now for days, months, more, there's been
nothing to make you shine as before. Then
one gray morning the final price arrives:
there in the blurring rain, a tuxedoed man waits
under a ragged, black umbrella. He takes

your arm and leads you to the subway steps, where
as you descend the worn, slippery stairs,
he waves himself away: goodbye.
Continuing down alone, you find
your eyes and nose adjust to darkest air.

And out of distant darkness comes the train to collect
its load. You'll ride it into the headlight path
that disappears after each cold, sweeping flash, which
relentless, pursues the endless tunnel to its
farthest unlit corner, the one you'll never see.

WHAT I'M DOING IS

I'm blowing my newly hyphenated life wide open
like those dinnerplate-sized magnolias so
expanded on shiny-leafed laden branches
weighing themselves down into dipping
deep over the wall I haven't yet climbed.
They come from the half-hidden other-side garden,
opening from creamy fists into
blossoms bigger than the most open-palmed hand
so welcoming that it would never be a smack.

This is the South they keep telling me and
not just crape myrtle sprawls but even bugs bloom bigger
everywhere, breaking through the scrawl of heat
as the season just explodes
these nights in parking lots where red tail lights
of dark-windowed cars tear off
kicking up the dusty gravel and what sounds like
the heart-stopping crack of sprayed-back bullets,
really is.

FOUR

HOW IT BEGAN

We'd been freezing peas all day, my mother and me,
by evening I was hot and took off
to the carnival just set up outside of town.
Eighteen and ready to do anything that night
so long as it'd make me feel good, I stood on a hill
looking down into the pink and green lights, the spinning
machines, sweet and frying smells mixing. What I wanted
was a man's eyes to come right into me, make me
catch my breath, press my legs tight under my cotton
flowered dress. I'd never gone off with anyone yet. Up to that summer
there were two or three who kept me awake all hours
just by my thinking of the way their arms brushed
the back of my waist in passing by. And we didn't do more than that,
pass by and nod or smile a bit, I'd look away, my face warm.
Or I'd see one at the bar, his head tilted back, a beer
at his mouth, his neck arched in a clean line;
sometimes our eyes met in the mirror, and I'd turn embarrassed
by my thinking him close to me, our skin tight and touching.
The first night overlooking the crowd and noise I only watched.
It was a world made up of couples, circling the booths and tents,
their faces bright in the colored light.
The next night I walked right into it
saying hellos and returning glances, then let someone stroll me around,
buy me a soda, show me the fastest rides, then take me
to a place where the grass sank soft and deep, my body humming
and then our breathing hard together, little moans in between, soon
my legs wrapped high around him bringing him closer than anyone had
been; then everything slower, more quiet, separate again.
It was easier after that—I could stand and
stare at who I wanted and know he wanted me,
and that I'd go. Mostly they weren't from around here and after visiting

the fair they'd be leaving. It didn't much matter, there'd always be
another to lie down with, our bodies never more alive,
as though it could somehow save us. Still,
nothing ever took away how nice I'd felt the time
I'd stood alone, looking down from the dark, excited
by that electric place below. It was like times
when my parents had gone in early and I'd sit on the step and
stare at the moon and listen to the crickets, while the breeze came up
and felt like a hand moving all over me until I'd shiver
and hug my arms close, wanting, not knowing what.

IN FLIGHT

I
Up here we believe in night,
trusting things to blacken
on schedule. And up here
nothing alters that:
once we've passed the sun
there's usually the moon dipping
and stars snapping into formation.

There is also the chance
no planet will bother with us:
the wing disappears; blindness
joins our vocabulary, as does terror. Sometimes
there's no one down there.

II
Above your town, I consider
bailing out. I perch at the plane's edge,
then enter the swirl of night clouds. Falling,
the sky sliding by like hair,
I search for a sign of light.

Your cows will bring me in,
lifting their white faces
where it's safe to land.

FINDING A PLACE ON THE COAST

I see you standing
by the yellow house above the sea
in yellow November light.
The wind befriends your coat;
you look around yourself
the way a child tests his foot in
the print left in mud, where
someone passed before him.
This stretch of grass and salt air
edged by blue, and more blue,
surround you, though you've not yet decided
how they fit. Watching from the car,
what could I call to you: Look
there is a man and a building
and it will soon be winter; but for now
he and the world
welcome each other, like parts
of one body, preparing itself
for the first step.

WAITING FOR YOU

The doctors have machines that tell me
you're really in there: at four months, I listen
as your tiny heart flutters
twice as fast as my own; or it's flickering whitely
on the screen, while your watery shape
flips and bats, like a sea-mammal, lost
from all the others.

You show up afterward,
in the sonic photograph, floating
pale and prehistoric. It appears that you, also
live in loneliness, separate from the man
who has forgotten
how hard he talked
to keep us.

Lately at night, when he looks over at me,
I turn away, waiting
for the first *tap tap tapping*. I know it will mean
you're with me, you're finally with me.

LETTER NEVER SENT

Finally spring today
here in the Northeast. Seven robins
listen for worms
and tip into the greening grass.
I watch at the window. Starlings
dive with cries
that mimic a baby. The child growing in my body
sometimes feels like a hand reaching deep
to all my secrets. There, it's always winter.

Today, because it was
spring and I was walking
by the bay, I forgot direction
and remembered our past by that other ocean.
Soon I believed you were the one waiting
at the house, might even be the one
to know the place that hand explores.

Now, in this room
seeing another sunset reflected in water,
I should turn,
and you should be standing behind me.
I continue counting birds, and face west
where there's just sky
preparing for evening.

SONG FOR A CARGO SHIP

Midnight, the fog disappears,
and pacing the sleeping house
I see across the water
a freighter, its levels lit
like a carnival city.
Those foreign sailors waiting for port
must wonder at our darkened town.
For me, these hours
bring no peace. A husband
who snores, a child who wakes in fear,
parents who've suddenly aged.
This time I'm shipping out. Joining the crew
on their journey, I'll learn the language;
concoct meals of iridescent fish; then dance on deck
all night in summery white,
while the sea keeps settling around us. Now
I'm gathering my records of international
folk songs, my bird whistles from eight countries;
now I stand on shore
with an armful of beach roses, waving
my straw hat like a flag. I shout greetings.
Soon they'll let the lifeboat down; soon
we'll be lifting anchor.

DRIVING AROUND

I
A man stands in front of his white-fenced lawn
watering the sidewalk. Although in the noise of traffic
you can't hear him, you see he's whistling. He's no one
you'll ever know. Older than your father, he looks ordinary
in his tan bermudas, green polo shirt. Behind him
the last shrunken lilacs are discolored, coppery,
but the peonies open into full flower, white, pink, and pinker.
The various bushes check off the days, the Northeast summer dwindling
with each new blooming, each falling of petals into clipped grass.
You're only passing in a car, yet the drawing in
of cheeks and lips, the eyes calmly watching the spray of water
spattering the concrete, all let you know the man is pleased by his world.
As you pass by on your way to get your daughter from the pool, you're aware
that when you forget the man's face, you'll still remember
the fact of the whistling, the garden
dependably marking off the season, and your thoughts seeming to be
those of an orderly, settled life, of
the kind of adulthood your parents wanted for you.

II
Years before, because you wanted to live somewhere you'd never lived,
you moved somewhere you knew no one. It was almost winter
in that Northwest city and your room was cold enough
to show your breath as you lay awake and lonely.
You drove around a lot in your old gray Dodge,
mainly at night. The threat of black ice
kept you from traveling the many hills and bridges too quickly.
You'd been told the road wouldn't shine until the instant
your wheels lost control, and then you'd catch that glistening
like the bad smile, coming out of the dark, of someone who will hurt you.

Mostly there wasn't much traffic, you listened to the radio,
thinking you might never talk to another human being again, might
always be listening to something coming from a distance.
Months later, just before spring,
your money ran out. And though you'd earned the first blooms
as much as anyone, you went back to a warmer place, sold the car, forgot
those AM country songs; but then one would sneak up on you and hum,
from far away yet close as someone whistling right into your ear, giving you
shivers the same way memory of any dead past
can suddenly, wake up and stretch a bit inside you.
For a moment you'd believe only
that you were off on some piece of pavement
going much faster than you should.

III
This afternoon at the pool as you wait in the car
with the groceries, and your life appears
orderly and settled and you only go driving to arrive somewhere,
you know that the kind of adulthood your parents never
wanted for you has never left you. Often
a sudden nudge from the past will surprise you: you're sure that
in the hills it's hot and dry tonight. You find yourself young again,
happy to ride on the back of his motorcycle, holding him
around the waist of his smooth shirt, so white
in the blue time of dusk. The dip and rise
of the bike around the road's wide curves is like dancing,
you think. The air seems to be moving through you,
warm and even, and as the two of you climb
the sky gets closer and this time you're certain
you'll lift easily into that glowing place
that just goes on and on.

BIRDS

You've become lovers with a friend's wife.
You tell no one, fearing that otherwise
your lives will break apart, the pieces
come flying at you
like leaves whipping across the wet road at night. Last night
going home after seeing her again
and trying not to think what
her husband, your wife, others, might do
if they knew of your meetings, those leaves
flew up to your windshield so fast,
at first you believed they were birds. And
you ducked your head, nearly swerved; then felt foolish
for behaving as though that could stop
real birds from hitting a window.

You know this kind of secret
loving makes separations, finally,
for everyone it touches; works like the wind
driving those leaves so they seem to change
into birds, colliding with your vision.
If you could keep calm, not react. If
you could keep eyes open, not even
blink. If you could catch the leaves
even as they transform, feathered and breathing,
hold them in your hands,
and then convince them somehow to begin singing, until
they all together lift into flight, lifting
the two of you out of your lives
together, with them.

ADULTERY

I

Because we are outlaws, where you take me this night
the moon has no face, its surface smooth
as the snow shaping the hills and valley
outside the car. We park off a road rarely traveled
this time of year. Dark pines and thin silvery trees
throw shadows on your face lowering to meet mine;
we make love, wrapped in heavy coats,
knees bumping glove box and seatback.
But still we can see each other clearly, moonlight
everywhere, hitting snow, the chrome of fender and door.
From within this blinding whiteness I think
we are as perfect as the landscape that contains us.

II

Those mornings when we woke together
it was always snowing. The flakes fell thick
and silent to white ground.
That's the only color I remember: white
smoke between us in dark bars, white flicker
of t.v. in off-season motels, the white knot of our hands
beneath tables, across car seats,
our bodies close and white in the clandestine
places we met all winter.
It's an old story: two people belonging to others.
New feelings covered us the way
trees weighted with fresh snow become beautiful.
And though we knew the year's whiteness would disappear,
giving way to spring's yellows and greens,
we imagined even that difference
as a gift to us from the world. We imagined those colors
withheld till they grew tired of hiding, as we did.

But people aren't trees waiting for warmer
weather to bring back the shape of leaves and branches.
Only we can change our lives. We need to want, then
do; or else remain like passive objects in landscape:
cold; for a time less cold; and finally, cold again.

IN DECEMBER

Outside the house
yellow grass stands
stiff and ragged with
new snow; sky of no color
grows darker all morning.
By the fire you read
of a city in Spain, a city
of eternal spring, where
mild breezes carry the scent
from hundreds of orange groves, until
the pungent fruit ripens, and bowls fill
on every table. Reading,
you remember the small
California town where you lived
as a girl. There also
citrus blossoms whitened
the air; lemon trees
lined the streets, winding
even up into the hills: tiny flowers
dropped down, so the sky
seemed constantly bright,
upon the lives below, calm
without winter. Here
outside the house
it will snow again and again. You'll sit
reading of Valencia, thinking
of your girlhood, and let
that other whiteness drift and fall,
fragrant around you.

TRAVELOGUE

We've come a long way
to avoid another winter, a long way
to speak a language not our own.
Taking a bus to the beach outside the city, we find
a narrow strip of sand that winds for miles
fronted by aging, pink hotels.
Many dead things have washed up here:
battered fruit, empty bottles, broken plastic toys,
entire palm fronds, wooden crates smashed by waves,
all ending amidst the tangle of weeds
and shiny green flies hovering in the warm, March air.
Skirting the surf, my shoe barely misses
a huge dead rat, grayer for the damp;
and from beneath another mound of trash
jut the hind legs, curls dingy, of a sheep.

While we walk through the garbage that rode in
with the tides, what nearly rides out is the baby, asleep
in his carriage. The foam unexpectedly reaches where
we've parked him, turned away from his first real sun,
and threatens to carry him off. Washed away
drifting out farther and farther in his yellow craft,
he would continue to sleep, oblivious.
Better then if he never woke
to believe in the crisp line of horizon as rescue.
We learn too soon of the illusion, learn that the line keeps
pulling everything adrift
into its false promises, but never gets closer
and none of us ever land.
And for each believer hopefully sailing off,
there's something sent back: the rotten oranges
bobbing in dirty water that rushes toward our feet,

toward our still sleeping child,
toward all who've come
to watch the sea gather and spill.

IN MOURNING

I

In Spain, the women in black mourn many deaths:
parents, husband, a child
young or grown. It's really death in general
that makes them fold up all their bright clothes
from the very first loss. The blue skirt,
yellow blouse, are put away
as if each garment stood for someone loved.
The men too have shed their colors. In gray
or brown felt hats, they slouch in groups
in the square, standing against white walls
strung with bougainvillea, trailing scarlet, magenta, orange.
Though they stand apart from the women,
they're just as separate from the vines of flowers,
keep the same memories
in the low brims' shadows around their eyes.

II

This year both of my parents lost their mothers.
I had a baby boy, never seen
by his great-grandmothers. My mother believes
although it's sad these three cannot meet,
I have replaced a bit of the family, have repaired
the grief through the birth of a child. But I think
of the Spanish, and their constant mourning,
and in loving my son, I also begin
to mourn for him. In giving birth to him
I have made his death true, put it with my parents', my husband's,
mine. Each morning buttoning pink dress or violet shirt, I wear a lie.

III

In Spain, children bring the country joy. Yet
it's children the dark clothes are worn for:
deaths of the past who were once children;
the children of the present
who are the deaths of the future. In Spain
a woman in black steps from a shop to stroke
and coo at my laughing, fair *niño*. And across the street
I see two men, grin and nod, grin and nod.

SEVILLA

To the blue and white blanket where you sit
under the trees with your pretty wife and baby, a breeze comes
after a storm threatens but passes by,
and it shakes out the fat, green leaves,
throwing about the scent of the citrus flowers
poking through like creamy white buttons.
The sky brightens, the day's cooled down, and the peacocks
who'd drawn their tails to a close, reconsider, circle the park, hint
at even more beautiful iridescence. Your afternoon suddenly
wraps itself around the three of you on the deep lawn
like a little dream can suffuse you with happiness in the seconds before
the clock will go off. Maybe nothing was right
before you slept; maybe waking will prove worse. Yet for a short while
you're beneath leafy branches that are not only in full bloom
but bear fruit at the same time. And this confuses you.
In your native northern climate, in orchards of cherry, apple, pear,
fruit follows flower, as cause and effect. To see both at once,
co-existent, seems impossibly lovely. If such a sight is common
it's not something you remember from your botany texts. It's not something
you would believe when you travel back from your visit here. Still, for now
you marvel at this scene: your family, together, amongst yellowest lemons,
and lemon blossoms. And as in sleep, you don't anticipate the certainty of
time's impertinent alarm: how soon
it announces itself, and the dream's end;
or that you set it yourself and will always do so.

FIVE

SURVIVAL

The thing you've dreaded most
has happened: someone gone, you never imagined
the how of going on. Oh you should know by now it's the dead
rusted needles that make the dry pine smell we like.
Discover that fact by simple sight,
simplicity of the newborn, of mere
acknowledging breath: simple
to possess only that. Certainly more simple than the child

describing the circus: *it was loud*
and we clapped our hands. Least simple
the adult being driven
through northern summer's short season:
could you slow down a bit
I really like this
and it's going too fast for me.

You ought to know by now what the infant grows
to forget: we love to witness the plain
skid and crunch and tang
of November leaves, all the dying
we can't hold back. We even
send them to the final smoke
that sharpens the air, and that, though it burns
our eyes and lungs, we walk through at evening
as it twists up beyond us,
and we breathe deep that waste, that ache.

TREADING WATER

Never having been a swimmer,
you're here dangling, afloat.
On the muddy bank, where your toes
gripped a last hold, then slid,
a boy stands and slits one fish
while still eyeing his pole.
The farther out you bob, the more certain you are
his gaze forsakes you.
You're also lost to the man
whose arms curve over the surface
and carry his long body, upstream.
Every limb holds you buoyant,
away from this river's bottom, those weeds
that will coil tighter against struggle.
What you'd feared most
was your lungs forgetting air,
and your muscles finally claiming their repose,
but no one warned that the neck is supported
by the current, the easy caress
to which you could give yourself.

YOUR WINTER'S TALE

Begin with the ice,
its scattered ticking
against the window, all night
you hear that *tick*
tick, tick, alone.
So what that one man stayed
more than a few seasons, you had his child—so
what.

Now the dark hours make a bad sound;
you'd forgotten how that happens.
You try to scare it off.
You bring home men
from the bars where you go
to dance your loneliness out.
Any man who sweats, and keeps step,
you keep; hope he'll keep away
that glittering noise.

They all breathe your name, and
sweetheart; but after they all sleep easily,
right through, leaving you behind.
You're lying awake
and listening to nothing more than water
frozen and blown at glass. Still, it ticks: *late*
too late; so what, so what.
End with the ice.

FAMILY PLOT

We talk to the dead with stones;
My mother shows me the way, gathering
small rocks loosened from earth
and grass. We place them, leave
a message, on each slab
that marks a grave,
for someone gone.
This is how my mother speaks
to her parents now; she looks
as if she'll fly away, her arms
flapping in black coat sleeves,
mouth opening in protest
like a baby bird whose own mother
circles in a sky too far off, too long.
Shhhh, I say, *shhhh*, and smoothe
her feathers, hold her down.
We kneel and read the names,
piling on pebbles, anything
resembling rock. I find
there's a lot to say to the dead,
to keep the living here.

ROAD REPORTS

I

Today the men are out working on the road,
repairing the winter's holes with tar and gravel.
This doesn't mean the season has softened much. But
because we drive everywhere in this far northern place,
the world gets broken beneath us and the weight
of months of ice and snow. These road crew patches bring only
short term relief from the bumps and dips
our cars carry us through. Still, the men with their
yellow caution signs, orange trucks and shovels,
digging, filling, and smoothing, comfort me,
like a lover's palm smoothes
my hair back, the lines of my forehead away. Then also,
while I imagine no promise, I feel certain
what's difficult will always ease.

II

Since we have no streetlamps, here the nights surround us
with a darker dark; we depend on stars, the moon,
to light our way. On cloudy nights without that help
we don't see past our own headlights unless, rarely,
another car approaches or we round a curve
to find the red glow of tail lights. What's strangest
is the emptiness in the rearview mirror, a blackness
that seems like absolute nothing, although it can't be so.
Those times are like a life out of context: no memory
of any past, and no sense of possibility or the future.
Yet if the road unexpectedly drops off,
at least what's unimagined, unseen, can cause no fear,
so loses its power to harm, while behind
there's no sign to remind us that anything ever did.

III

In the backcountry where the roads are rough, less clear,
the ways are edged by fields, endless as ocean, and blanked out
by snow so deep it buries the fences.
Some of that snowy flatness does hide bodies of water: streams, lakes,
rivers. Sometimes a hot spring shows through
with the contrast of its black, steaming shape.
A car could go off the road at dark and not know if it will hit
ground or ice, nor whether the latter is solid, will even hold.
A driver may not imagine what may be waiting beneath that white sheet,
start to pass wildly, and continue
in a sidelong slide across the span where
not a tree stands to stop him. The place he lands
may be merely a colder cold to dig out from,
or the coldest cold that keeps.

IV

The coldest night of the year
driving home on the river road we turn off our lights,
the moon's so bright; the thick columns of mist
winding up the icy cliffs off of the half-frozen water
are luminous the way we once were taught ghosts are. These days
the glowing white swirls don't frighten us.
Now we ask questions about why parts of a river freeze hard
then stop in a clean line where whitewater still rushes.
These questions all have scientific answers, being physical phenomena,
though we don't know them. We pull off the road to watch,
stop talking, and the moonlit car fills with an inexplicable calm;
but as we watch, this feeling becomes as natural in its mystery
as the light held in river smoke
traveling from one shining surface to another.

LULLABY

Climb to the top of a house
where your children are sleeping
under the eaves like tucked in
sparrows. *Safe and sound*
is what you whisper as you
kneel down beside them to hear
their tiny breaths resound.
This is what you're here for:
to keep them so, blanketed as long
as anyone ever can, against
the world's rough surface, the world's
careless hold. You don't remember
your own mother and father, yet
they once bent above you and
settled the covers just as though
that could keep you from harm
beyond the nights you'd spend
under their roof, their protection.
How little did you know, but
they knew, as you know now, and
yours will too. And all of you
leaning over with the same soothing
kiss, give the gift of illusion, which,
when broken, can at least be passed on
as a token, a little lie to ease
the way, until the child says goodbye
and sets off to find what he's blessedly
been kept from being shown.

THE FOREST

Younger and in love, I recited
the names of the warblers,
their twitterings and tweets
of the piney morning, I heard
through the verdant circle
surrounding my clearing
where the world was shining.
I never imagined
the eventual cooling shadow
that falls over such places,
how the birds withdraw
their voices into shade,
and that this is what life
can be made of: sometimes
music and sunlight draw around us
like it was meant to be;
and then the warmth fades
as slowly as a cloud crosses
a windless sky; and we watch for awhile
until we believe bad weather
will never pass by.
Of course it does; and again
we recall the lark, thrush, yellow wing,
all returned to the ear
yet not the view, as we don't see
anything, just the sweep of green
obscuring the identity of each singer,
their different colored markings.

It's when the sun gets covered
we should look:
living things are at our feet,

visible, on the ground,
unfolding, growing, digging down.
They didn't gather for us;
they're just around. And when
love is gone, they quietly
go about their existence,
being good ordinary company.
In their plain silence
I've learned their names
and though they don't answer in song,
they don't abandon these woods
when the skies inevitably change.

SEEING

Here's perfection, through glass;
the silence seems to harness
pure vision to its task
of looking at, into, not through,
a landscape remarkable and plain
in its spectrums and shapes of greens:
a hill, a curve of grass, a grove
of trees, ivy-climbed brick,
all as handsome and solid
as anything ever seen.
The other senses might make
much more of the scene, adding
song of birds, voices of girls
at play, scent of mown field, touch
of warm breeze lifting one's hair.
And yet, it's fair to say
this wall of window brings to bear
a separate focus upon the world
out there, and only this
cutoff way is wholly seeing.

LOOKING AT MAPS

It's better not to go back to
the plazas washed with early sun, scatter
of pigeons, and a few figures, heads down,
criss-crossing in diagonal pursuits, or to

the winding drives on mountain passes,
pausing at the brink above
the blue sea, the broadside below
flush with brightness.

How luxurious the time of
days plump with light that blinds, nights
artificial with color, neon illuminating
any spot that might darken and hide;

harshness was tempered the way wild iris covers
and surrounds the crumbling ruins, green softens the rock
angles that everywhere abound, and flowers pop
up to smoothe uneven ground. It is better

not to go back. What seems from afar
paradise remembered, has its visitors and inhabitants
missing as if dead, the way it will be when
from everything we've everyone not merely left, but gone.

SPRING

One day you wake up, there are
flowers on the trees, leaves
will be next. You let out
your last breath, tell your wife
you've got new reasons
to live, not leave your life
like the boy who left his shadow,
a gray nylon cut-out of his shape
he couldn't stick back on with soap,
though god knows he tried.
What stitches the spirit to your own
shoulders as a parachuting cape
is the unexpected *deja vu* as buds break
open into colors on even the most stubbed out
stumps of plants. Like you and love,
they'd nearly disappeared from the path,
without resistance, in a wintry world of
only trash swirled about by cold, bad air and
the shuffle of people's feet they've
forgotten to lift from the street.

CROSS COUNTRY AT NIGHT

—for my father

Nothing seems to be living
but the highway, splitting the sweep of cool fields.
The world is fastened by a breeze of damp hay
and the dry, glowing storms of summer.
Dead animals litter the road's edge.

Stopping,
there will be the print of white stripe
on the eye's next encounters.
Now, it's all center line.
Yet the heat lightning on the horizon brings something to mind:

a young girl somewhere, quietly opens the screen door to
stand outside with the father, who holds her
and makes a lesson from the sky's pale flashes,
of weather and distance, and also of silence.
Remembered later, this will be about scale:
a solitary figure, amidst the dark stretching on every side.

MORNINGS

Back then, there was the shiny
air and grass from the dew
when you were three, playing under
the Japanese maple and the milkman stopped
in his van to chat with your mother.
Bright times continued. The ocean encircled your
next town like blue-green glass; it might have
invented those broken bottle scraps, smooth and
luminescent, you collected from its beach.
Mornings sing good promises when they begin
in such ways. They kept them sometimes
even as you shifted from place to place.

This is why you walk
along the gravel road today at the right
time for that still, wet light to surround
you and it does, but not how it was.
Your memory replays all the other days
that luckily started the same, with the grass
or sand fresh and untrammeled, held under
some not too harsh sun that was kinder than
it would later become and the world as ragged
with it. You can't concentrate with these
recollections unfolding before you like scenery
on a painted, paper fan. You imagine standing
in a sort of meadow and discovering the shadows
of your history had left no crush or stain
on the soft stalks waving and shimmering.
You lie on your back: even with eyes closed
here is the only spot you are; as if with a new
lover, it could be the very first time,
and you could start again.

BOATING

A woman is rowing her
husband and child around
the lake, under a coming-
upon-evening sky. People
on the shore and in
speedboats laugh and call out.
It's funny to see
the wife pulling the oars
while the family gets a ride.
To her, dipping and leaning,
feeling the seemingly infinite
green beneath them, it's fine.
This is how she sees her life:

the way gets radiant or cloudy,
dark and then light; she follows
a crooked line of her own mind,
sometimes caught in the waves
of a motorboat's backwash, other
times setting a trail of clear calm.
Her passengers sometimes chide her,
offer advice on where to avoid, shout
she's going wrong. But she believes
she was made for this, the rhythm
as she bends herself forward and back,
reaching toward the water's shifting
destinations, sometimes heeding
the others' commands, yet never letting
the tools of steering and passage
leave her strong and steady hands.

IN SUMMER

Only last night, the sea seemed frozen; I could have left
my life, walked across to some other. And the moon
passed through clouds that filled the sky the way
ice floes bridge a river.
My breath on the window was shaped like a door.

Now tonight, the softest
air, firefly sparks over the field, each
convince me of July. It really is
July, and a moon smoothes the ocean's surface
until the water laps the beach
as calmly as a lake
in summer. Everything comes loose.
I no longer invent escape, but welcome
this time and place, as the thrush
calling bell-like, invites another dawn.

ON THE ROAD TO BLUE EARTH

This Minnesota sky is bigger than a place
like heaven. How much we love
a journey with no visible end,
feeling the moment extend, as earlier
when we discovered heat's singular sound
contained in the rising pitch of cicadas
drilling the still afternoon while we watched
the horse move dreamlike up the slope toward
the apple trees where the fruit fell
with a succession of small, harmless thuds
outside our window. Now, driving
beneath the grown dusk inflates that
sudden, suffusing pleasure and this one too,
to eternity—always the sun
hovering in the mirror, the corn
saluting greenly, the black spread
of peat grounding the sweet waft
of grasses sliding past, and the evening
insects *crea-creaking* like a constant rotation
of sprinklers blessing and preserving
our view of cool fields beyond
the exit signs we can pass by,
without ever passing on.

IN THIS DREAM

We are always dancing:
you lift your arms above me
like a bird in a summery place.
Sometimes there is music
and the softest shadows;
other times the air carries us
through the rhythm of tall, flat buildings,
bright and steady in full sun.

How easily our bodies converse:
they compose songs, moving
now in unison, now
in complex and perfect harmonies.
We let them go. As they move
they leave everything else behind.

A RED TRACTOR

Today I watched a young boy, his jacket fallen beside him,
watching something over a gray fence. I could see
a red tractor parked in a field of dead March grass.
The boy stood on tip-toes, on the bottom rail, just looking
at that wonderful, overgrown toy. He didn't notice
when I idled the car behind him, or when I drove on.

I think about this last day of a month when
winter's left behind and spring's still
too far ahead, like that machine we can't climb on
unless someone will offer us a ride, and we know they won't.
But we stand right there, as though expecting
the engine to start going, and the ground to begin turning over
rich and dark, ready for planting.

It's not weather or seasons I'm really thinking about,
merely the time of year, in a year of big changes,
when the best, most awaited change is about to happen,
yet seems more remote than in all the months before. We see it
sitting right over there, the same as spring, the same
as that red tractor; and we can only stare at it over a fence.
Where would it take us anyway, just around that old
patch of dirt. Still, then it would begin to rumble and dig
and what we'd been hoping for would come through at last,
newer and greener than in any year past,
at least that's what we'd say as we sat high up
on the tarnished seat, having been lifted to it
exactly like we'd been waiting for all along.

ACKNOWLEDGEMENTS

Thanks to: Bernard Meisler for his support over the years; Dorette Amell for sharing her beautiful painting *Main Street* (photographed by Jay York;) Jeff Thorneycroft for his friendship, patience, creativity, and hard work in bringing my cover vision into being; Ptolemy Tompkins; Gina Frary Bacon; Emery Dobyns and Mara Rose Lieber; and last, but never least, David Conrad for always going beyond the call.

ABOUT THE AUTHOR

Rebecca Weiner Tompkins has been published in many literary journals (some under Rebecca Weiner,) including *Ploughshares, Poetry magazine, Pequod, Seneca Review, Sensitive Skin, and The Antioch Review*. She received a grant from the NEH, a college Academy of American Poets Prize, several City University of New York Creative Incentive awards, and in 2016 a poetry fellowship/sabbatical from Manhattan Community College, CUNY, where she is a tenured professor of writing and literature, currently on leave. Her B.A. is in Poetry from the College of Creative Studies, UC Santa Barbara, her MFA is from Goddard College, and she is ABD from the PhD Program in English, The Graduate Center, CUNY.

For several years she was the instructor of The Wild Angels Writing Group, at The Cathedral Congregation of St. Saviour, Cathedral of St. John the Divine. Since 2009 she has taught various seminars on the intersection of theology and poetry/poetics at The Church of St. Mary the Virgin, NYC where she serves as the deacon. In 2010 she presented a TEDx talk, "Sensing Convergences," at University of Kent, Canterbury, Kent, UK.

Additionally, she is an acoustic and electric violinist who has recorded and performed in NYC, Nashville, and Europe with, among others, Patti Smith, Scott McClatchy, The Sometime Boys, Emily Duff, Life in a Blender, Conrad y Skordalia, Maynard and The Musties, Sergio Webb, and Mark Huff.

She has two children, Mara Rose Lieber and Emery Dobyns, and two grandchildren, Louis Eggleston Dobyns and Florence Devoe Dobyns. These days she splits her time between New York City and Nashville.

Also available from **SENSITIVE SKIN:**

A Change in the Weather
poems by Ron Kolm

"Open these pages and join Ron Kolm, arch-denizen of New York City, as he picks his way through the lethal and potentially surreal. In Kolm's world, dada is a verb and anything is possible in the mope-eyed bookstores and dystopic subway darknesses he traverses. Expect the unexpected. Charles Bukowski throws shade on Velvet Underground."

–George Wallace, author of *Poppin Johnny* and *Who's Handling Your Aubergines*

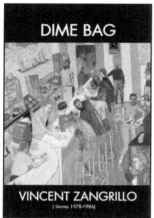

Dime Bag
stories 1978–1986 by Vincent Zangrillo

"If the streets of New York could talk, they would want Vincent Zangrillo to be their voice. The smell of the match under the spoon, the voices shouting two apartments down, a sigh lost in the rush of 10 million people hustling to get through their day, these are the things Zangrillo knows, cherishes and tells. We are blessed to have his unblighted vision of the damned."

—Tom Graves, author of *Pullers and Crossroads: The Life and Afterlife of Bluesman Robert Johnson.*

Why Sing?
poems by John J. Trause

"The range and playfulness of Why Sing? answers that question in a variety of lyrical modes. Trause is a one-man orchestra. Anyone who knows who Felix Paul Greve is and quotes him in German is an imp who knows much and isn't shy about taking his singing babes into the agora."

–Andrei Codrescu, author of *The Art of Forgetting*

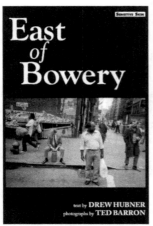

East of Bowery
stories by Drew Hubner / photographs by Ted Barron

"Drew Hubner's prose and Ted Barron's photos are kin, at once raw and lyrical, grit and grace, which is what the city was like back then. The combination is magic, the essence of the time and place."

—Luc Sante, author of *Low Life* and *Kill All Your Darlings*

Paris Scratch
snapshots of everyday Paris life, by bart plantenga

"A marvelous book – imagine Baudelaire taking a camera and throwing out his pens and precious inks in a rebellious anti-anti-Dadaist manner, then taking snapshots of everything that comes his way ... the author's camera moves very fast, the 'center cannot hold' and we live only twice!"

—Nina Zivancevic author of *Death of NYC*

NY Sin Phoney in Face Flat Minor
snapshots of everyday New York life, by bart plantenga

"Look carefully at these written snapshots to see what lurks below the surface & don't be surprised if you feel a bit self-conscious, frightened, even nauseous at times."

—steve dalachinsky, PEN Award author of *The Final Nite & Other Poems*

Backwards the Drowned Go Dreaming
a novel by Carl Watson

"[Watson] writes like someone who pushed himself to the wall, then pushed through it to the void and came back with stories to tell. Here he reclaims the Seventies, one of the more desolate of recent epochs, with the clarity of Proust, the balefulness of Bodenheim, and the raw honesty of an Iggy song."

—John Strausbaugh, author of *Black Like You* and *Sissy Nation*

Music: Drawing Down the Muse
drawings by David West

"West's talent is of visual emotional representation; from eye to hand to heart. Through these works on paper- ink, guache and color pencil, we become mesmerized by the focused immersion into sound."

—Karen Finley, *Shock Treatment, A Different Kind of Intimacy*

Barefoot in the Heart: Remembering Neem Karoli Baba
an oral history, edited by Keshav Das

"Barefoot in the Heart is a divine raft to take us across the ocean of darkness to the glorious land of light. Every page is filled with Maharajji's nectar..... Profound gratitude to Keshav Das and his collaborators...."

—Jai Uttal

Border Crossings
poems by Thaddeus Rutkowski

"There is an eerie and edgy appeal to Rutkowski's spare poems and in his sly, deadpan humor as he takes potshots at an absurdist world. Sometimes playful, ultimately serious, the poet brings an unusual heritage—Polish and Chinese—to his observations. One ends up cheering this poet's curiosity and humanity, wanting more stories, more poems."

—Colette Inez, author of *The Luba Poems*

Mayakovsky Maximum Access
selected poems by Vladimir Mayakovsky
translated with commentary by Jenny Wade

"Jenny Wade's vibrant translations of Vladimir Mayakovsky's selected poetry offer an outstandingly energetic and insightful view into the work of one of Russia's most fascinating, towering poetic (anti)heroes. Rendered in vivid, passionate language, this volume is a page-turner, while the detailed commentary that accompanies every poem provides nuanced insight into the mind of the great poet and into the intricacies of his innovative use of the Russian language."

—Anton Yakolev, author of *Ordinary Impalers*

For more information about these and other books, go to:

www.sensitiveskinmagazine.com/sensitive-skin-books

CPSIA information can be obtained
at www.ICGtesting.com
Printed in the USA
FSHW021511210121
77747FS